21ST CENTURY SCIENCE

DRUG
RESISTANCE

By Caroline Green

Tick Tock Direct

ISBN: 978 1 84898 107 2 pbk

Copyright © TickTock Entertainment Ltd 2011
First published in Great Britain in 2011 by TickTock,
The Pantiles Chambers, 85 High Street, Tunbridge Wells,
Kent, TN1 1XP

Printed in China
9 8 7 6 5 4 3 2

Picture credits (t=top; b=bottom; c=centre; OFC= outside front cover; OBC=outside back cover)

Hazel Appleton, Centre for Infections/Health Protection Agency/Science Photo: 41b
Library. Thierry Berrod, Mona Lisa Production/Science Photo Library: 44t. Borderlands/Alamy:
42–43. Andy Crump, TDR, WHO/Science Photo Library: 57b. Design Pics Inc./Alamy: 50t. A.B.
Dowsett/Science Photo Library: 6–7t, 12t. Reza Estakhrian/Getty Images: 29t. David R.
Frazier/Science Photo Library: 30-31. Steve Gschmeissner/Science Photo Library: 6b. Paul
Gunning/Science Photo Library: 39t. Imagebroker/Alamy: 37. iStock: 3B (and throughout), 8–9, 27b,
35t, 55b, 56. Dr Kari Lounatmaa/Science Photo Library: 28. Philippe Plailly/Eurelios/Science Photo
Library: 61. Philippe Psaila/Science Photo Library: 47. Phil Matt/AgstockUSA/Science Photo
Library: 32t. Science Photo Library: 53. Shutterstock: OFC, 1 (all and throughout), 3 D/E/H (and
throughout), 4–5, 10–11, 13, 22, 23b, 24–25, 26t, 34–35b, 40t, 45b, 49b, 58t, 59t. Science
Source/Science Photo Library: 14t, 15t, 18t, 33t. Scott Sinklier/AgstockUSA/Science Photo Library:
54. SSPL via Getty Images: 20b, 21b. St Mary's Hospital Medical School/Science Photo Library:
19b. Mark Thomas/Science Photo Library: 51b. Geoff Tompkinson/Science Photo Library: 16–17,
38t. Sotiris Zafeiris/Science Photo Library: 48.

Every effort has been made to trace copyright holders, and we apologize in advance for
any omissions. We would be pleased to insert the appropriate acknowledgements
in any subsequent edition of this publication.

The author has asserted her right to be identified as the author of this book in
accordance with the Copyright, Design and Patents Act, 1988.

NOTE TO READERS
The website addresses are correct at the time of publishing. However, due to the ever-changing
nature of the Internet, websites and content may change. Some websites can contain links that are
unsuitable for children. The publisher is not responsible for changes in content or website
addresses. We advise that Internet searches should be supervised by an adult.

A RETURN TO THE DARK AGES?

IMAGINE THIS. ON A MONDAY MORNING A MAN IS SCRATCHED ON THE FINGER BY HIS PET CAT. THE FINGER STARTS TO SWELL AND WEEP PUS ON WEDNESDAY. BY FRIDAY, THE MAN HAS A RAGING TEMPERATURE AND IS ADMITTED TO HOSPITAL. BY SUNDAY, HE IS DEAD.

FIGHTING TO LIVE

It sounds like something from a horror film, but before **antibiotics** were discovered, people caught deadly infections from simple everyday wounds. The availability of antibiotics ushered in a whole new era, when humans could at last control harmful bugs. Other medical breakthroughs followed over the next decades, with the development of **vaccines** against killer **diseases** and the discovery of powerful drugs against **malaria**, a major cause of death in the developing world.

In fact, there was such a wave of optimism that experts began to predict a time when infectious diseases would be entirely wiped out. In 1978, scientists from 134 countries held the International Conference on Primary Health Care in Alma-Ata, Kazakhstan. The conference had an ambitious aim – 'health for all' – and concluded that 'an acceptable level of health for all the people of the world by the year 2000 can be attained'.

Yet, in the 21st century, 17 million people are still dying from infectious disease every day, according to the World Health Organization. Around 90 per cent of these deaths are caused by just a handful of diseases. Six deadly infectious diseases — pneumonia, tuberculosis, diarrhoeal diseases, malaria, measles and HIV/AIDS — account for half of all premature deaths, killing mostly children and young adults. And drug resistance is a major factor in relation to most of these diseases.

Modern medicine and treatments mean that most young people in the West grow up healthy and happy. However, there is still a lot of work to be done, particularly in the developing world, to control diseases that kill.

THE BUGS FIGHT BACK

Today it is possible to treat illnesses that would have meant certain death even 20 years ago. Doctors have a whole arsenal of drugs to use against the **pathogens** that can make us sick. But the pathogens are fighting back and drugs that once cured are increasingly becoming useless. Pathogens are micro-organisms, or microbes, that cause disease. We often use the words 'bug' or 'germ', but pathogen is the correct term.

HOW DRUG RESISTANCE WORKS

All living things adapt to their surroundings and find ways to survive when changes occur in their world. Pathogens are no different. All pathogens make millions of copies of themselves every day. But not every single copy is exactly the same as the last, and there are always small, random differences known as **mutations**. Some of these mutations will be able to resist the effects of drugs that would

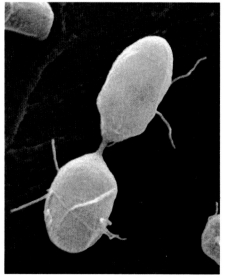

Bacteria multiply rapidly by dividing. Here, a salmonella bacterium, which can cause food poisoning, is creating two new daughter cells.

In equatorial Africa, Ebola fever is an often fatal illness that is caused by the Ebola virus (above). There have been a number of outbreaks since 1976.

normally have killed the **virus**, just because they have slightly different characteristics that are not targeted. Eventually, these mutations may outnumber those that the drug was effective against and when this happens, the drug stops working. Even more worryingly, pathogens often become resistant not to just one of the drugs that is used to treat a particular disease, but to all the drugs available. That is known as multi-drug resistance.

The situation is serious. Not only are new and hard-to-treat diseases or conditions appearing, but some old foes are coming back with a vengeance. There is also the threat of terrorist attacks that may use once-beaten diseases such as smallpox in biological weapons.

A CAREER IN SCIENCE

Vanessa D'Costa is a PhD student in biochemistry at McMaster University in Ontario, Canada. She also did her undergraduate work at McMaster.

A DAY IN THE LIFE OF ...

Vanessa D'Costa is based in a lab at the McMaster Health Services Center, a hospital on campus. She is currently looking into antibiotic resistance in soil and how this may provide information for predicting the way that resistance works in humans in clinical practice.
It has been established that soil bacteria has become resistant to environmental pressures in ways that are similar to those mechanisms found in drug resistance.

THE SCIENTIST SAYS ...

"What excites me about this work is that it may one day help us to predict clinical resistance before it happens. By studying these new environmental mechanisms, we can not only develop diagnostic techniques, but also establish ways to circumvent the resistance, allowing us to think one step ahead of the antibiotic-resistant bacteria."

REVENGE OF THE 'SUPERBUGS'

There have been lots of stories in the news about so-called 'superbugs'. These usually refer to a bacterium known as **MRSA** (methicillin-resistant-staphylococcus aureus), which has been responsible for many deaths, mainly in hospitals. But relative newcomers such as MRSA are only part of the story.

A RANGE OF DANGERS

There has been a rise in diseases that medical science believed to be controllable with the right drugs. **Tuberculosis** (TB) is one example. TB has existed for thousands of years, but in 1943 a highly effective antibiotic called streptomycin was discovered, and other successful drugs have been developed since. Today, strains of the bacteria that cause TB have found ways to resist these drugs.

This directly threatens millions of people in many parts of the world but also has huge implications for sufferers of the **HIV/AIDS** virus. HIV/AIDS weakens the immune system and increases the chances of getting TB. Worse still for HIV/AIDS sufferers, despite the success of a treatment with a range of drugs known as Anti-retroviral Therapy (ART) – the HIV-virus is also starting to show signs of developing resistance.

Malaria is another deadly enemy that is fighting to stay ahead of the game. Incredibly, it has been responsible for more deaths throughout history than any other disease. Scientists originally believed the only solution was to wipe out the mosquito parasites that carry the disease, but this proved to be impossible.

The female *Anopheles* sp. mosquito bites into human skin. The parasite responsible for malaria is carried in her saliva.

So, instead, doctors focused on finding medicines to treat it. A drug called Cloroquin looked like the solution, but in the 1960s, doctors realized that malaria was becoming resistant to the drug. It took just ten years for resistant strains of malaria to spread from one area of Thailand to the whole of Asia, Africa and South America. Newer drugs have all shown signs of resistance as well, including artemisinin, which was being hailed as the magic bullet for malaria only 15 years ago.

Today, drug resistance threatens not only the health of us all, but the notion that humans are superior to the bugs that share our planet.

INVESTIGATING THE EVIDENCE: TB AND LIFESTYLE

The investigation: Poverty is known to be associated with TB, but why is this the case? Scientists have investigated the lifestyle of both TB patients and people who do not have TB who are living in Liverpool, England.

The scientists: A team led by Professor Peter Davies, head of the TB Research Unit at the Cardiothoracic Centre, Liverpool. He is also Secretary of TB Alert, a charity that supports TB projects around the world and promotes awareness of the illness.

Collecting the evidence: The evidence was gathered by visiting people in their homes and compiling information on a wide range of lifestyle factors, including diet, travel and living arrangements.

The conclusion: An analysis of the data showed that a diet that includes fresh fruit and vegetables and dairy products appears to have a protective effect against contracting TB or having the active form of the disease. The biggest risk factor for infection was visiting countries such as India and southern Africa. Smoking was also found to play a part in death rates from the disease, and smokers with latent TB were more likely to die from the disease.

CHAPTER ONE

THE WORLD OF THE MICROBE

A TEEMING MASS OF LIFE EXISTS ALL AROUND US EVERY MOMENT OF OUR LIVES, YET WE ARE BARELY AWARE THAT IT IS THERE. WE MAY LIKE TO BELIEVE WE ARE IN CHARGE OF THIS PLANET, BUT MICROBES ARE THE TRUE MASTERS. SOME THRIVE IN THE MOST EXTREME TEMPERATURES THAT THE EARTH HAS TO OFFER. SOME NEED OXYGEN TO SURVIVE JUST AS WE DO, BUT OTHERS CAN EXIST WITHOUT IT. WELCOME TO A WORLD WHERE THE MINUSCULE RULES.

Viruses are so tiny that you need a microscope to see them. The protein shell that surrounds their genetic core attaches itself to target cells in the body, which it then attacks.

WHAT ARE MICROBES?

Microbes are tiny **organisms** that we can only see with the aid of a **microscope**. They are everywhere: inside and outside our bodies, on everything we can see, and in places we cannot. They live inside and on all plants and animals.

It is estimated that the first microbial life on Earth existed around 3,500 million years ago, compared with the 'mere' 195,000 years since humans appeared.

There are four main kinds of microbe. They are known as bacteria, viruses, **fungi** and **protozoa**. Bacteria are creatures made up of just one cell and are so small that 1,000 in a row could fit across the rubber on your pencil.

Viruses are even tinier. They are technically not 'alive' at all because they cannot exist in their own right. Consisting of little more than genetic material surrounded by a coat of protein, they invade living cells and almost always cause disease. Viruses can even infect bacteria.

Fungi are a type of plant that, unlike other plants, cannot make their own food. They can be single-celled or multi-cellular. The types of fungi we know best are mushrooms, **yeast** and **moulds**, but around half are microscopic varieties that can cause disease in humans. Other types can help us and are used in food preparation or the making of certain medicines.

Protozoa are one-celled creatures that may be parasites and can cause disease in humans. Malaria is caused by a protozoan parasite.

E. coli, here dividing and multiplying, is a bacteria that normally lives in our gut. It can be picked up accidentally, particularly if we do not wash our hands properly, and may cause health problems.

SHARING THE WORLD

The overwhelming majority of the microbes on our planet either live alongside us in harmony or actively work for us in some beneficial way. Only a tiny fraction – about one per cent – are harmful.

Around one hundred thousand billion bacteria are living on and inside your body right now. In fact, you are made up of more microbial cells than human ones. The gut alone is home to about 1kg of bacteria – more than the total number of people who have ever lived on the planet. Most of these microbes are 'friendly'. In other words, they work to protect us against other, more harmful organisms. In our stomachs, they play a very important role. They break down food and help us to digest it so that we can get all the **nutrients** we need to keep healthy. The bacteria that work for us are called **commensals**.

BACTERIA AND VIRUSES

The bacteria that harm us are very much in the minority and are known as pathogenic bacteria. We may breathe them in, or get them from direct contact. Or we may eat them if we do not cook or wash certain food properly. Bacteria that normally live inside us without causing trouble can also cause severe health problems if we accidentally ingest them. Bacteria can cause different problems in different parts of the human body. Streptococcus pneumonia affects the lungs, but is also responsible for ear infections. Some bacteria may be harmful to humans but not to plants and animals, and vice versa.

Viruses are even harder to fight than bacteria, because they do not live independently. They have to hijack other living cells to exist. You will probably have made a home for a rhinovirus hundreds of times. This is the virus that is responsible for the common cold.

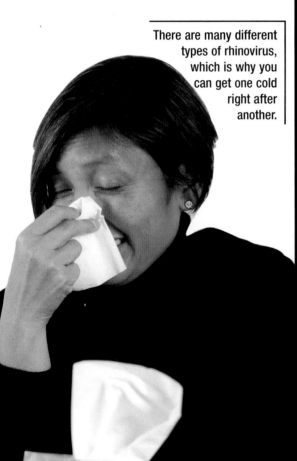

There are many different types of rhinovirus, which is why you can get one cold right after another.

A CAREER IN SCIENCE

Richard James is Professor of Microbiology and director of the Centre for Healthcare Associated Infections at the University of Nottingham in the UK. During his PhD in Microbiology at the Middlesex Hospital Medical School, he studied the bacterium E.coli. His focus now is on developing new antibiotics that are active against hospital 'superbugs' such as MRSA and developing rapid diagnostic techniques to identify them.

A DAY IN THE LIFE ...

Professor James directs other researchers in laboratory work, where they grow bacteria, clone and sequence genes, and look at the potential of antibiotics for killing bacteria. The university has recently set up a facility for whole genome sequencing so that, when a patient has a very serious infection, they can isolate the bacteria and determine its complete genome sequence to help understand how it is capable of causing such infections. This is the first step in developing better diagnostics to identify rapidly such bacteria in other patients and new antibiotics to be able to treat patients.

A SCIENTIST SAYS ...

"I enjoy being able to discuss the results being generated by the researchers in my laboratory. Giving live media interviews, such as on the BBC news, is a bit scary but also fun."

This is a computer model of the structure of a protein from a TB bacterium. By studying the structure of a bacterium, scientists can find out how quickly the bacterium is mutating.

EVOLUTION OVER TIME

Drug resistance is **evolution** in action. All living things have to adapt to the environment in which they live – even humans. Over time, we may evolve certain genetic traits that can protect us against illness. For example, in areas where a disease such as malaria is rife, a minority of people may become **resistant** to certain strains. But in the human world this is a very slow process that takes many generations to occur, if it happens at all.

Genes have to be passed on from parent to child, with around 25 years on average in between.

Evolution is a much faster process when it comes to microbes. One bacterial cell can become two in just 15 minutes, two can become four in 30 minutes and so on. If they did not have to cope with any environmental limitations, such as starvation and other microbes, they could cover the surface of Earth in almost no time.

All forms of microbe are able to develop resistance to drugs that are designed to kill them. This process of fighting back is known as 'selective pressure'. It always involves genetic changes, for instance by sharing or acquiring new genetic material.

The bacterium that caused the Great Plague in Britain in 1665, travelled throughout Asia, the Middle East and other parts of Europe.

GLOBAL MOVEMENT

Bacteria do not need a long-haul flight on an aeroplane to get across the world, although the increase in global travel does help them to hitch a ride. Even more worryingly, scientists have discovered in recent years that microbes are not only capable of picking up mutations from their own genetic family. It seems they can swap and pick them up from other microbes as well. This is a global gene pool, or as some scientists have put it, a kind of genetic lending library. Pathogens can pick up new traits all the time that help them to survive. This means that they can find ways to resist drugs designed to beat them.

INVESTIGATING THE EVIDENCE: HOW TO BEAT TB

The investigation: A team of scientists looked at the mechanisms of the mycobacterium responsible for TB, which is increasingly resistant to drugs.

The scientists: A team led by Professor Johnjoe McFadden of the School of Biomedical and Molecular Sciences at Surrey University, UK. The team liaised with other bodies, including the Biotechnology and Biological Services Research Council (BBSRC) and the Health Protection Agency in the UK.

Collecting the evidence: McFadden and his team used computer modelling to analyze the pathways used by the **latent** or 'sleeping' form of the disease. People with latent TB can go on to develop the active illness and become sick. Even while the disease is active and causing symptoms, latent bacteria remain in the body.

The conclusion: Growing cultures of the latent bacteria in the lab takes a long time and does not allow the scientists to analyze it in the human body. The computer modelling has allowed them to build up a picture of mechanisms that the bacteria use and these will help ultimately to find drugs that will target them more accurately.

CHAPTER TWO

DEVELOPMENT OF ANTIBIOTICS

ANTIBIOTICS HAVE BEEN DESCRIBED AS THE SINGLE MOST IMPORTANT DISCOVERY IN THE HISTORY OF MEDICINE. THEY HAVE CERTAINLY REVOLUTIONIZED HEALTHCARE ACROSS THE WORLD. BUT THEY HAVE ALSO CREATED NEW PROBLEMS IN WAYS THAT WERE NEVER FULLY ANTICIPATED BY SCIENTISTS.

THE GOLDEN AGE

Bacteria and fungi protect themselves from other microbes by producing substances that are poisonous to their enemies. These substances are antibiotics. Naturally occurring antibiotics existed on Earth about three billion years before humans.

Almost all of us have taken a drug form of antibiotic at some time in our lives. They are prescribed for bacterial infections in any part of the body, but most commonly the throat, ear or **respiratory system**. They are also used in farming.

No antibiotic is capable of wiping out all the harmful bugs in one fell swoop. They work by killing off the weakest bugs first – including some that have not been making you ill –

and leaving behind stronger and resistant bacteria. If you do not take the full course of an antibiotic, you leave the strongest bacteria, and this can lead to them developing resistance to the original drug.

There are more than 150 varieties of antibiotic on the market today. In many countries, antibiotics are only available on prescription from a doctor. However, in many parts of the world, they can be easily bought over the counter. It is also possible to buy antibiotics from the Internet. This means that many people are taking them without any input or advice from a doctor.

A scientist innoculates a series of culture medium plates with bacteria, as part of research into new forms of antibiotics.

16

Alexander Fleming (1881–1955) was a biologist and pharmacologist at St Mary's Hospital in London. He received a Nobel Prize with Chain and Florey for their work with penicillin.

THE DISCOVERY OF ANTIBIOTICS

A Dutch merchant called Anton Van Leeuwenhoek (1632–1723), was the first person to see bacteria using his homemade microscope. But it was not until the middle of the 19th century that scientists agreed that these microbes could be responsible for disease. This led to the question of whether some bacteria could cure as well as kill. In 1877, Louis Pasteur, a French chemist and **microbiologist**, made a major breakthrough when he discovered that anthrax, a highly infectious bacterial disease, could be cured in animals by injecting soil bacteria. Other developments followed over the next few decades but no one could find a way to make a medicine from the bacteria that was not harmful to humans.

Then, in 1928, the British scientist Alexander Fleming made a chance discovery that changed the history of medicine. Returning to his laboratory after the weekend, he discovered some scientific plates containing the Staphylococcus bacteria had become mouldy. The surprising part was that some of the bacteria were now dead. Fleming realized that the fungus growing on the plate was creating a substance that was poisonous to the bacteria. He called the substance 'penicillin'.

Unfortunately, Fleming could not find a way to extract the penicillin and turn it into a meaningful treatment. By 1941, scientists Howard Florey and Ernst Chain managed to grow enough to treat a policeman with a life-threatening illness. They injected him with penicillin and his recovery was at first almost miraculous. However, they did not have a big enough dose to stop the infection from coming back, and he died.

This is the original culture plate of the fungus *Penicillium notatum* made by Alexander Fleming at St Mary's Hospital in 1928.

INVESTIGATING THE EVIDENCE: MICROBES AND DRUG RESISTANCE

The investigation: A team is carrying out research into patterns of drug resistance in various microbes, including bacteria, viruses, fungi and parasites such as malaria-transmitting mosquitoes. They are analyzing new drug resistance and tracking the increase or decrease in established resistances.

The scientists: Dr Berit Müller-Pebody of the Department of Healthcare Associated Infection & Antimicrobial Resistance Centre for Infections at the Health Protection Agency in the UK, with many different departments of the HPA and outside hospitals, laboratories and research facilities.

Collecting the evidence: Information is taken from a huge database called LabBase, which contains reports of all micro-organisms retrieved from patients in almost 400 hospitals and laboratories in England and Wales.

The conclusion: Infection control strategies (such as isolating certain infected patients) have resulted in a levelling off of MRSA infections. But new resistances are being discovered in which traditional medicines have been effective, and resistance also being found in anti-virals and anti-fungals.

THE GOLDEN AGE OF ANTIBIOTICS

As better methods of production were found, the so-called 'miracle drug' penicillin gradually became available to the mass market. For the first time in history, humans were able to claim superiority over the microbial world. However, this did not happen overnight.

THE COCOANUT GROVE FIRE

After Howard Florey and Ernst Chain's successes were reported in the medical press, scientists for the US military began working in secret to try to produce the drug to treat wounded soldiers. On 28 November 1942, a fire broke out at a popular nightclub in Boston called Cocoanut Grove. Inadequate safety provisions and overcrowding – more than twice as many people were packed into the club than was allowed by law – meant that within just 15 minutes the building was an inferno. In total, 492 people died and the lives of another 200 hung in the balance.

One of the biggest dangers for burn victims is infection. The military realized that it was time to test the new drug, and many lives were saved. But it was not until the following year that penicillin hit the news.

GOING PUBLIC

A father whose baby daughter was dying of a staphylococcal blood infection

Tubes of penicillin were easily transportable to wherever they were needed.

contacted a major US newspaper to beg for help. The editor smelled a good story and publicly challenged the body that looked after the still small supply of the drug to provide the penicillin. A car owned by the newspaper helped deliver the drug amid huge fanfare. The baby girl lived, the national press picked up the story and before long, heartfelt pleas were pouring in from all over the country for access to the drug. By 1952, it became available on prescription in the UK and USA. Before long, around 907,000kg of penicillin were being produced each year in the United States alone.

These women are working on a production line for pencillin in Liverpool, UK, in 1954.

The investigation: Could a susbtance from soil called streptomycin kill the bacterium responsible for tuberculosis?

The scientists: Dr Selman A. Waksman (1888–1973) of Rutgers University, New Jersey, USA, and his team of students had isolated streptomycin from soil brought in by a local farmer. Waksman's student, Albert Schatz (1922–2005), is believed to have done much of the work behind the discovery.

Collecting the evidence: Waksman and Schatz believed that streptomycin was active against the TB, but did not have the means to test their theory. They supplied the research institution the Mayo Clinic, based in Minnesota, USA, with the substance to test it, first on guinea pigs and then on human patients.

The conclusion: Streptomycin was found to be a powerful drug against the bacterium that causes TB and a range of other diseases. The drug made a huge profit for the company that developed it, but within a short space of time it became apparent that bacteria could quickly develop resistance.

Antibiotic eye drops were used successfully on a mass scale against the eye infection trachome, which affected up to 400 million people worldwide.

A WAVE OF OPTIMISM

Over the next few decades, other types of antibiotic were discovered, such as chloramphenicol, which is still in use today. Researchers also began to look beyond naturally occurring antibiotics and found ways to make synthetic versions of these life-saving medicines in the laboratory.

PREVENTION RATHER THAN CURE

There were other major breakthroughs happening in medicine during this period. For the first time, bodies such as the **WHO** (World Health Organization), founded in 1948, began to look at not just treating disease on a grand scale, but at how to prevent it in the first place. Mass health programmes were launched, including one targeting a tropical infection called yaws, which attacks the skin, bones and joints. Penicillin virtually eradicated the disease in Asia for a time.

Mass vaccination programmes were put in place against TB, and leprosy also became widely treatable for the first time. There was great hope about wiping out malaria as well, thanks to a new drug called choloroquin and spraying the mosquitoes with the chemical **DDT**.

Doctors began to imagine a time when all infectious diseases could be conquered. In 1969, William H. Stewart, the US Surgeon General, made a bold statement to Congress: 'The time has come to close the book on infectious disease.'

But it was a false optimism. Even in the earliest days of antibiotics there were warning voices about taking drugs for granted and using them improperly. Alexander Fleming himself told *The New York Times*: 'The greatest possible evil in self-medication is the use of too small doses so that instead of clearing up infection, the microbes are educated to resist penicillin and a host of penicillin-fast organisms.' It would be a long time before the world would heed that warning.

Today, synthetic versions of many antibiotics can be manufactured quickly and easily.

INVESTIGATING THE EVIDENCE: RESISTANCE PATTERNS

The investigation: Scientists wanted to find out exactly how large the environmental level of antibiotic resistance is in locations with high and low human activity.

The scientists: Dr Mirva Drobni, the molecular biologist working on antibiotic resistance in the Department of Medical Sciences/Infectious Diseases at Uppsala University, Sweden, together with Professor Bjørn Olsen, also of Uppsala University.

Collecting the evidence: The team looked at environmental dissemination of bacterial antibiotic resistance that has a human source. They used cotton swabs to collect faecal samples from birds in different locations. The bacterial material was then analyzed back in the laboratory and the scientists looked at which antibiotics the birds were resistant to. With those that showed resistance, the team then found out which genes may be involved in the process.

The conclusion: The team found that bacteria carried by birds in close proximity to human activity tend to display the same resistance patterns, and the same genetic variants as are found in human clinical samples in that region. Studies like this are important for understanding the mechanisms underlying bacterial resistance.

CHAPTER THREE

DNA (deoxyribonucleic acid) is found in the nuclei of all cells. The acid is made up of phosphates, bases and sugars and is in the shape of a double helix that is slightly twisted.

MICROBES FIGHT BACK

JUST A FEW YEARS AFTER THE FIRST USE OF PENICILLIN, SCIENTISTS AT ONE LONDON HOSPITAL DISCOVERED THAT 14 PER CENT OF STRAINS WERE ALREADY RESISTANT TO ANTIBIOTICS. BY 1946, IN THE SAME HOSPITAL, RESISTANCE WAS AS HIGH AS 59 PER CENT.

BACTERIAL MUTATION

Bacteria mutate to resist environmental threats, such as medicines, in three ways. First, they may mutate spontaneously. This means that the **DNA** – the genetic material that determines all the characteristics of the bacteria – changes on its own. Second, a bacterium may pick up DNA from another bacterium in a mutation process called 'transformation'. The third and most unpredictable kind of mutation, however, is when resistance is acquired from a small circle of DNA known as a **plasmid**. Plasmids multiply within bacteria and can move between different species, causing resistance to multiple drug therapies. They can only be seen with very powerful machines called electron microscopes.

VIRAL MUTATION

It is not just bacteria that mutate and learn how to evade the antibiotics or synthetic drugs that are designed to kill them. Viruses have only one purpose and that is to reproduce. Genetic mutations usually occur by accident as the virus makes copies of itself. These can make them more resistant to protective mechanisms such as antibodies. As to other much larger microbes, the *Plasmodium falciparum* parasite that causes malaria has a highly complex **genome**, or collection of genes. Its ability to adapt and 'hide' from the body's immune system has made it very hard to treat, especially as it can mutate to resist the drugs targeting it.

THE MISUSE OF ANTIBIOTICS

Although antibiotics were thought to be a saviour of humankind, they were taken for granted and have been used in the wrong way for decades. Now their efficiency is seriously threatened and we face the real prospect of a return to the days before their discovery.

RESISTANCE

The precise mechanisms of how pathogens become resistant are not clear.

In the 1980s, medical research turned its focus to other kinds of drug development and there was little work being carried out on new antibiotics. Resistant strains of microbe were developing all the time, but the attitude prevailed that, if needed, there were always other antibiotics available. Today, there is resistance to almost all forms of antibiotic.

Many doctors say that

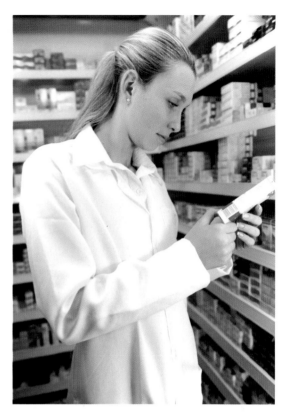

In many countries, antibiotics can be simply bought over the counter, without prescription.

patient expectation is one major factor. They report that many people come into surgeries with symptoms of a viral infection such as a cold, sore throat or earache, and demand antibiotics to clear it up. If someone will not take no for an answer, it is often easier for the doctor just to write a prescription. This causes more harm than good. The medicine will not play any role in the person getting better, because their body will fight off the bug by itself, but the patient is left with the impression that the drug has done its job.

Even when antibiotics are prescribed as they should be, if they are not taken properly, we as consumers are giving resistant strains a helping hand. The patient usually starts to feel better before the drug has been able to target all the relevant bacteria, and this leaves behind resistant microbes that are then passed on within a community. It has been estimated that over half of the antibiotics used worldwide have been bought privately, and half of those are typically used for just one day's treatment. The consequences are serious. Antibiotic resistant strains of just one bacteria, *Staphylococcus aureus*, have increased by eight per cent in a year.

Today, it is increasingly easy for people to order prescription drugs over the Internet.

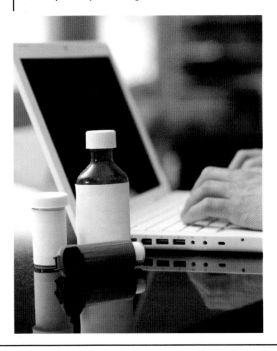

A CAREER IN SCIENCE

Dr Alan Johnson is a clinical scientist – in other words, he is a specialist who does research and advises other scientists on the approach to a treatment that is most likely to be successful. Dr Johnson's first degree was in biological science, and his interest in how microbes cause disease led him to specialize in medical microbiology. He is now Head of the Antimicrobial Resistance Section of the Health Protection Agency in the UK.

A DAY IN THE LIFE OF ...

In his earlier career, Dr Johnson was lab-based, but now he mainly works at a computer, collecting and analyzing data. He is currently involved in studying a number of antibiotic-resistant bacteria, including MRSA. He is particularly interested in how MRSA can cause bloodstream infections in children. Occasionally Dr Johnson gives lectures about his findings, both in the UK and other countries.

A SCIENTIST SAYS ...

"For me, the best thing about being a scientist is that I get to spend each day doing something I enjoy and I actually get paid for it. Also, working in the medical field means that we can, hopefully, help to improve the well-being of patients."

This colour magnification shows a cluster of MRSA bacteria dividing. This potentially deadly bug is common in hospitals, infecting the wounds of patients.

GETTING ILL IN HOSPITAL

Hospitals have become a major focus for the problem of antibiotic resistance. In many countries, the media have highlighted this aspect of the issue more than any other. So why are hospitals targeted by the so-called 'superbugs'?

FIGHTING A SUPERBUG

'Superbug' is a term that is normally used to refer to a bacterium known as *Methicillin resistant staphylococcus aureus*, or MRSA. It is a pathogen that is not only resistant to *methicillin*, but all the other common antibiotics that once treated it, such as penicillin, *flucoxacillin* and *cephalosporin*. It is even showing signs of becoming resistant to *vancomycin* – the drug of last resort.

Hospitals are a prime target for the development of resistant strains of microbe. After all, they are places where there are lots of people in close contact with each other. Anywhere that humans are in confined proximity gives pathogens the opportunity to spread quickly. By their very nature, hospitals contain lots of different bugs, but this is not as straightforward an explanation as you might expect. Although it is easy to suppose that, because there

INVESTIGATING THE EVIDENCE: PREVENTING MRSA

The investigation: Scientists wanted to find out if it was possible to develop a vaccine to prevent MRSA infections, and establish why infections recur in 25 per cent of cases, when people are usually immune to getting an infection once they have had it.

The scientists: Professor Gerald Pier, Dr Tomas Maira-Litran, Dr Jean Lee and Dr David Skurnik, all of Harvard Medical School in the USA.

Collecting the evidence: The team identified a molecule on the surface of the MRSA bacterial cells that can be purified and injected into mice. This allowed them to see, using blood tests, if the process caused the animal to make protective antibodies. If so, the antibodies are capable of killing the MRSA bacterial cells. This would mean that the mice would not get an MRSA infection.

The conclusion so far: The team discovered that they must change the surface molecule chemically in the lab in order to make it capable of inducing antibodies that kill MRSA bacteria and protect against infection. Good results so far have set the stage for making and testing the vaccine in humans and animals.

It is vital that everyone in contact with patients washes or cleans their hands thoroughly.

are lots of sick people, there are more bacteria, it is actually visitors who are believed to be the prime carriers of the microbes.

However, people in hospitals are more vulnerable and likely to pick up opportunistic pathogens for several reasons. They may have wounds from surgery and other procedures, and these provide an inviting entry point. Patients are more likely to be elderly and frail, or simply in a state when their natural **immunity** – the ability to fight off bugs naturally – is at a lower level than usual. Doctors are even finding now that with certain cancers, it is not the disease that ultimately kills someone, but the fact that the **chemotherapy** has left them open to ordinary infections.

CHAPTER FOUR

RESISTANCE AND THE ENVIRONMENT

IT IS NOT JUST THE HUMAN CONSUMPTION OF ANTIBIOTICS THAT HAS LED TO THE DEVELOPMENT OF RESISTANCE. ANTIBIOTICS HAVE ALSO BEEN HEAVILY USED IN FARMING, AND THIS HAS RESULTED IN MAJOR IMPLICATIONS FOR HUMAN HEALTH.

TREATING ANIMALS FOR PRODUCTIVITY

Animals are prey to a range of bacterial infections just like humans, and farmers soon realized that the results in treating certain animal diseases were impressive. However, since the 1950s, the drugs have been used not just to cure infections, but also to promote animal growth. Today, low doses are still added to the feed given to livestock. The idea is that the drugs prevent low-level diseases in the animal. And using antibiotics in livestock also means that animals can be reared more intensively, with stocks kept packed together in close proximity without infections spreading quickly.

In 1969, a committee of scientists warned the world of the 'real and potential danger' that overuse of antibiotics in animals would help speed up the rate at which bacteria learned to resist drugs. Some antibiotics have even been banned in Europe and the USA. But, despite this, the combined use for **therapeutic** and growth promotion has continued to grow, according to the US pressure group The Pew Campaign on Human Health and Industrial Farming, which reports that animal production accounts for 70 per cent of the antibiotics used in the USA. Experts believe that this is helping to add to the 'resistance pool' of microbes, releasing them into the environment where they can grow and become stronger.

Antibiotics are usually added to the feed of animals such as cattle, pigs, sheep and chickens.

Farmers routinely ask vets to inject cattle with antibiotics to prevent illness and increase profitability. However, this results in drug-resistant germs being passed on to humans.

THE ENVIRONMENTAL CONNECTION

Most animal bacteria cannot survive in humans and therefore do not present a health threat. However, certain microbes are capable of causing severe and even deadly stomach upsets. There is increasing evidence that resistant forms of these have come about because of the way antibiotics have been used in farming. *Salmonella* is a bacterium that lives in the gut of animals, birds and humans, but if it is accidentally eaten, the infection can be spread by excreted bacteria long after all the symptoms have cleared up. *Campylobacter* is another pathogen that can be dangerous to humans, and causes similar symptoms. Both can lead to fatal conditions such as septicaemia, a type of blood poisoning. Another dangerous microbe that can live in both humans and animals is *Escherida coli* or *E. coli*, which can cause kidney damage and be fatal.

HAZARDOUS FOOD

Food poisoning affects an estimated 40 million people worldwide very year, according to the World Health Organization (WHO). icrobiologists believe that the use of antibiotics in farming is

Here, *Salmonella typhimurium* bacteria (green) invades human cells.

a major contributing factor to the number of food poisoning cases worldwide. A study by scientists at University of Georgia, USA, found that bacteria with resistance to common antibiotics was high even in chickens reared without the drugs. It is possible that this resistance is actually being carried in the genes from the birds' parents.

There have been many calls for a ban on antibiotic use for growth promotion. Some experts say that without antibiotics in farming, humans will be under a bigger threat from disease-causing microbes. But it seems clear that the over-use of antibiotics is causing a rise in infections that may not respond to the only weapons that we have left.

A CAREER IN SCI

Dr Arthur Thompson is the G.
Leader of Salmonella Molecu
Microbiology at the Institute
Research [IFR] in Norwich, U
has been at the IFR since 199
and has set up state of the ar
facilities to study bacterial ge
involved in infection. He is nov
concentrating on researching
the *Salmonella* bacteria.

A DAY IN THE LIFE OF ...

Dr Thompson and his colleagues are working to determine the genetic programming that causes *Salmonella* to become virulent. They want to establish which nutrients *Salmonella* needs for infection. This work has led to a patent for a vaccine. A typical day is spent drafting publications and proposals for further research as well as advising other scientists.

THE SCIENTIST SAYS ...

"It's exciting and rewarding to discover new things. This for me is the 'get out of bed' factor! Over the past decade or so, pathogenic *Salmonella* strains have started to become resistant to multiple antibiotics in animals and humans, which constitutes a major future threat to animal and human health. Hence, there is a need to continually develop novel therapeutic strategies."

Microbes are very good at clinging on, so hands need to be scrubbed in the thorough way required of doctors and nurses in hospitals if bacteria are to be washed off.

IS THE WORLD 'ANTIBACTERIAL CRAZY'?

Take a look in any supermarket and you will see a mind-boggling array of different anti-bacterial products. In the USA – the biggest consumer worldwide – they account for around $1bn sales annually. When swine flu was first reported in the UK, sales of the products soared by an incredible 279 per cent.

Antibacterial products usually contain chemicals that are capable of killing off some bacteria and viruses. However, in soap, for example, this is only true if hands are thoroughly washed over several minutes. The average person washes their hands for 3–5 seconds. which is simply not enough.

While a few of the microbes are washed off, plenty remain.

EVERYDAY USE

Studies are showing that 7 per cent of a particular *Listeria* bacteria, which causes severe stomach upsets, are now resistant to the ammonia compounds found in most cleaning products. Recently, some researchers in Japan discovered that the bacteria responsible for a particular kind of MRSA quickly evolved a resistance not only to antibacterial chemicals, but also to several antibiotics. This means that, in effect, people are helping the rise of resistant microbes by everyday actions involving household products.

Antibacterial products usually contain chemicals such as triclosan, triclocarbon and something called quaternary ammonium compounds, which are capable of killing off some bacteria and viruses.

INVESTIGATING THE EVIDENCE: THE DANGERS OF USA600

The investigation: The goal was to determine whether a certain strain of MRSA, called USA600, is more dangerous than others for patients infected with it.

The scientists: Team leader Carol Moore from the Henry Ford Hospital Division of Infectious Diseases in Detroit, USA, and Dr Marcus Zervos, Mary Beth Perri, Susan Donabedian, Nadia Haque, Dr Paola Osaki-Kiyan, Dr Anne Chen and Mei Lu.

Collecting the evidence: The team collected information about patients and the infection, especially whether or not the patients lived or died from the infection and how they were treated. The bacteria causing the infection was also collected and analyzed in the microbiology laboratory.

Conclusion: Patients who get infected with this strain of MRSA died five times more often than those infected with other strains that cause MRSA infection. The study found that 50 per cent of the patients infected with the strain died within 30 days compared to 11 per cent of patients infected with other MRSA strains. But the patients who got infected with the USA600 strain tended to be older and sicker, which complicates the statistics. The USA600 MRSA strain was found to be more resistant to antibiotics, such as vancomycin, usually used to treat MRSA.

CHAPTER FIVE

OLD ENEMIES, NEW INVADERS

IT IS ONE OF THE OLDEST KNOWN DISEASES BUT THERE WAS A TIME IN THE 20TH CENTURY WHEN EVERYONE BELIEVED TUBERCULOSIS COULD BE BEATEN. SO WHY IS TB STILL KILLING TWO MILLION PEOPLE WORLDWIDE EVERY YEAR?

BATTLING TB

The earliest documented case of TB was discovered in the spine of an Iron Age man, who died in around 300 BCE. TB remained a major global killer until the middle of the 20th century, when an effective antibiotic – streptomycin – was discovered. This, coupled with a vaccination known as BCG, meant the disease was controllable for the first time.

Since 1988, TB has been on the increase and in 1993, the WHO declared it a global emergency. Today, there are around nine million active cases worldwide.

TB is caused by the bacterium *Mycobacterium tuberculosis*, which gets into the lungs and **lymphatic system**. Over time, it can spread to other parts of the body and cause multiple symptoms.

Even if you do not get ill, you can carry it in what is known as a latent form. With the right combination of relatively cheap antibiotics taken over a period of time, TB is often completely curable.

Multi-drug resistant tuberculosis is known as **MDR-TB** and it has now been reported in 100 different countries or territories. The only drugs that can tackle it are much more expensive and dangerous, and have to be used for a longer time. TB also forms an unholy alliance with HIV/AIDS, because HIV/AIDS attacks the body's natural defences and allows TB to become active. It also appears that TB can speed up the HIV/AIDS rate of **replication**, and the amount of HIV virus in a person's system increases. It is still not known why this happens.

TB is rife in developing parts of the world, such as sub-Saharan Africa and southeast Asia, where most poor and malnourished people live.

This is a close-up view of the detector head of the Neotronics Olfactory Sensing Equipment (NOSE or e-NOSE, see box right), which detects contents of odours and aromas.

MRSA, SUPERBUG

MRSA stands for Methicillin-resistant *Staphylococcus aureus*. The last bit is the general name of the bacterium, and this particular strain is one that is resistant to the drug Methicillin, which once treated it. *S. aureus* is a bacterium that lives on the skin and in the nose. Around 30 per cent of the population carry it and it does not cause them problems. If, for example, you cut yourself and the wound starts to produce pus, then an *S. aureus* infection is likely to be the cause. In most cases, a person's immune system is able to fight off the threat, but in hospital, people are less able to combat the bacteria. MRSA is the most common cause of HAI (hospital-acquired infection). In the USA, it is estimated that one in twenty people visiting hospital will get a HAI and 90,000 will die each year.

MRSA

Antibiotics such as methicillin and flucloxacillin were able to beat these infections in the past. Today, the only treatment option is often an antibiotic called vancomycin, which is much

MRSA bacteria is carried around by about 30 per cent of people without causing symptoms.

The investigation: To find a novel technique that will allow hospitals to screen rapidly for bacterial infection. Conventional pathological laboratory-based methods are flawed because they are expensive and slow, resulting in delays and poorer care for infected patients.

The scientists: Dr Ritaban Dutta of Scensive Technologies Ltd, UK, working with various groups of doctors from different hospitals in the UK and India.

Collecting the evidence: The scientists looked into technology known as an electronic nose, or e-NOSE, that 'smells' bacteria. They wanted to find out if an e-NOSE could be used to sniff out certain bacterial infections. Six hundred patients infected with MRSA and two other bacterium were given swabs of the ear, nose and throat to collect samples. Dr Dutta developed an intelligent sensory system to pick up gases – or 'smells' – produced by the bacteria.

The conclusion: The e-NOSE was found to be successful in detecting infections in nearly 100 per cent of cases. It could correctly detect three strains of *Salmonella aureus* with more than 99 per cent accuracy. This work has led to a further investigation into how the device can be used.

more expensive and toxic to the patient. Since 2004, there have been cases resistant to Vancomycin – known as VRSA infections. This raises the frightening possibility of infections that we have no method of treating. Even with treatment, about 25 per cent of people infected with MRSA currently die – that is about 5,000 people a year.

MRSA can also occur, less seriously, outside a hospital setting. So-called community-acquired MRSA, or C-MRSA, has been found in otherwise healthy people who have not recently been in hospital or had courses of antibiotics. If caught early, it can be treated with antibiotics other than methicillin.

Long-haul flights are just one of the ways in which superbugs travel around the world. Whether people travel for their health or for tourism, there is a danger of infection.

EMERGING THREATS

Along with the existing threats from known enemies, new superbugs may emerge at any time as bacteria become resistant to first-line treatments. This may be partly because of the global nature of healthcare. People travel thousands of kilometres to have procedures such as cosmetic surgery in countries where they are less expensive. This can result in microbes being brought back to places where they did not previously exist. In settings such as hospitals, the microbes can quickly proliferate.

BUGS THAT TRAVEL

Hospitals in the USA, Canada, UK, Greece, France, China and South America have been reporting a rise in a type of bacteria known as *Enterobacteriaceae*. This bug is resistant to the standard antibiotic treatments used for severe infections – drugs that are called carbapanems and are seen as the drugs of last resort.

Enterobacteriaceae live harmlessly in the guts of many people without causing any problems. The carbapanem-resistant varieties are being carried to Europe from India, Pakistan, Turkey and other countries. They generally affect people whose immune system is vulnerable and can be fatal. Because there is no real treatment for

▶▶ www.hpa.org.uk/web/HPAweb&HPAwebStandard/HPAweb_C/1195733812122

infections of this kind, all hospitals can do is to be very vigilant in tracking cases. Guidelines are being issued stating that rigorous infection control procedures should be put in place if infections are identified.

Carbapanems are widely available in the Indian subcontinent, which is one of the main reasons why people's resistance to the drug has developed. The chances of picking up an infection like this in hospital are still small, say doctors, but it is important that careful monitoring takes place so that this bug does not become as widespread and dangerous as MRSA.

The *Enterobacteriaceae* have flagellae (hair-like strands) that are used for movement.

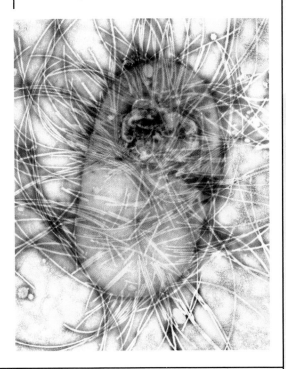

INVESTIGATING THE EVIDENCE: ANTIBIOTICS

The investigation: The aim of the research was to determine whether antibiotic resistance in environmental microbes had changed due to increased mass production and use of antibiotics since World War II.

The scientists: Prof David Graham, Newcastle University, UK; Dr Charles Knapp, Newcastle University (now at the University of Strathclyde); Dr Jan Dolfing, Newcastle University; Dr Phillip Ehlert, Wageningen University, The Netherlands.

Collecting the evidence: The team chose to work with soils because they retain usable DNA over long periods of time. They chose soils that spanned from 1940 to the present, extracting and categorizing DNA, using molecular biological methods to count genes in each soil sample that indicated potential antibiotic resistance.

The conclusion: They found that 78 per cent of the genes detected were increasing over time, especially in the last 20 years. This is important because increases in genes showing resistance to four major classes of antibiotics are used to treat disease in humans and animals.

Around 1,800 children contract the HIV/AIDS virus every day. This happens mainly in developing countries, and mainly by mother-to-child transmission.

HIV/AIDS

Today, around 33 million people worldwide are infected with HIV/AIDS. Caused by HIV (the human immunodeficiency virus), the disease kills or damages the body's immune system and gradually prevents it from being able to fight off infections and cancers. HIV/AIDS can be contracted in various ways, including sexual intercourse and via infected blood products, but can also be passed from mother to child.

Since the middle of the 1990s, a life-saving treatment known as anti-retroviral therapy has been in existence and this combines three or four different drugs that can inhibit the virus. **AART**, or HAART (highly active anti-retroviral therapy) is expensive. It works by targeting different parts of the virus through a 'cocktail' of drugs taken in combination.

Dr Brendan Larder is one of the world's leading experts in HIV drug resistance. He is currently chair of the Response Database Initiative research body in the UK, that monitors HIV resistance worldwide. He was largely responsible for discovering resistance to AZT drugs and also helped unravel the genetic basis of resistance.

A DAY IN THE LIFE OF ...

Larder spent 20 years working in laboratories, where he studied viruses such as HIV and analyzed their responses to different drugs. He also travelled throughout Europe and the USA.

THE SCIENTIST SAYS ...

"The first drugs developed to treat HIV were given to patients singly ('monotherapy'). Drug resistance occurred in every case where a patient only took one drug. This prompted us to think that treatment might be much more effective if more than one drug was given at a time ('combination therapy'). The development of safe and potent HIV drugs that can be given in combination has revolutionized the HIV/AIDS treatment area. The RDI, where I work now, is important in order to identify patterns of treatment success and failure. Then using this information, developed from building computer models, we hope to enhance and improve HIV treatment ."

But the virus is even becoming resistant to ART. The HIV virus replicates at a very fast rate. It mainly affects CD4 cells, which are important for immunity, by damaging them and preventing them from doing their job while helping the virus to replicate. Mutations do not occur because the virus is finding clever ways to beat the available drugs. The consequences are not just that infected people cannot be treated, but that they are able to pass on the new, highly resistant form of the virus to other people.

Pest controllers spray the pesticide DDT in a village in Madagascar. It was believed that DDT could be used to eradicate the *Anopheles* mosquito altogether.

MALARIA

Malaria kills more people than almost any other disease. It hits the very young more than any other group and a child dies from it somewhere every 30 seconds. Resistance to the drugs that are available are making it even harder to treat.

In 1880, a French doctor, Charles Louis Alphonse Laveran, discovered that malaria was caused by a single-celled protozoan parasite, *Plasmodium*, which is transmitted in the saliva of types of female mosquito. It can be picked up from an infected human and then passed on to someone else. It can also spread very quickly in areas where particular species of mosquito, mainly one called *Anopheles gambiae*, is prevalent. More than 90 per cent of cases are in sub-Saharan Africa. Poor living conditions, wars, the disintegration of health services and refugee movements all contribute to its existence.

Briefly in the last century, it was believed that wiping out the mosquito was the way forwards and a powerful chemical known as DDT was found to be an effective weapon against the parasite. Massive amounts were sprayed to kill the malarial mosquito. But the mosquito fought back. It was not long before mutations in the genes of the parasite allowed it to fight off the effects.

▶ ▶ www.who.int/topics/malaria/en/

Drug therapies were tried instead, and one called Cloroquin, that was first used to treat the disease in 1946, proved to be highly effective for many years. However, just one malaria parasite becoming resistant was all it took for a new strain of the disease to take off.

Since the 1970s, there have been at least seven new forms of antimalarial drug, but in each case resistance has developed, the drug is too expensive, or it causes too many **side-effects** to be a viable option. Artemisinin, originally from a Chinese herb, and its **derivatives** now have a 95 per cent cure rate. The WHO says the drugs must be used in a 'cocktail' with others – a little like the ART treatment for HIV/AIDS. But there are signs that resistance to the artemisinins is beginning in southeast Asia.

The parasite responsible for malaria is carried in the saliva of the female mosquito.

INVESTIGATING THE EVIDENCE: MALARIA

The investigation: To find out why *Anopheles* mosquitoes are so good at transmitting malaria. The mosquitoes must survive for 10–14 days to do so, and most do not live so long. This means a relatively small proportion are carrying the disease.

The scientists: A team led by Dr Peter Billingsley of the School of Biological Sciences at the University of Aberdeen in Scotland, working with scientists at the university and from other research bodies around the world.

Gathering the evidence: In the lab, the team maintain colonies of mosquitoes, and use them in a wide range of experiments. Collaborating scientists in the field collect the mosquitoes from different locations, using techniques that include satellite tracking systems to map movement.

The conclusion: Mosquito molecules play a vital role in transmitting malaria. By feeding antibodies to the mosquito, the team reduced its ability to transmit malaria. This technique makes it possible to reduce the insect's life expectancy, which further reduces its chances of transmitting malaria.

CHAPTER SIX

FINDING A SOLUTION

DRUG RESISTANCE IS A SERIOUS GLOBAL PROBLEM. IF THERE IS ANY CHANCE OF WINNING THIS BATTLE, EXPERTS MUST FIRST KNOW THEIR ENEMY. TO DO SO, THEY GATHER VITAL UP-TO-DATE INFORMATION ABOUT THE PATTERNS OF RESISTANCE WORLDWIDE.

NEW RESISTANCE

Just one drug-resistant microbe is all it takes for a new, difficult-to-treat strain of an infectious disease to spread. In these days of cheap and easy international travel, it is only a matter of time before a strain finds its way around the world. Experts need to monitor cases of drug-resistant infections and track their progress internationally.

In 1998, an organization called the Alliance for the Prudent Use of Antibiotics formed GAARD (the Global Advisory on Antibiotic Resistance Data). They brought together surveillance projects around the world and major bodies involved in infectious disease control, including the WHO and the US Centers for Disease Control.

In 2002, scientists found the first signs of resistance to an important class of drugs called quinolones in *Haemophilus influenzae*, a bacterium that causes pneumonia and meningitis (a dangerous inflammation of the brain and spinal cord). The discovery of a new resistant strain of this bacterium was a direct consequence of work by GAARD. People working in many locations around the world feed information directly to the scientists who are monitoring resistance. This information is used for educating the public and keeping track of the spread of resistance.

Today, EARSS (the European Antimicrobial Resistance Surveillance System), a surveillance and information system on bacterial resistance, links national networks throughout countries in Europe.

LA SCIENCE A B

Virologists have to wear full body protective suits when they are working with dangerous virus samples in the laboratory.

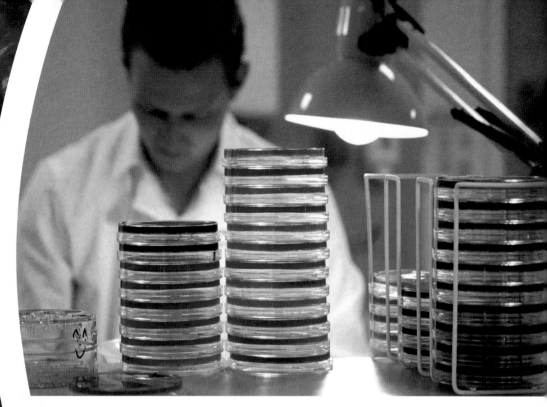

Laboratory technicians culture samples from patients in order to identify the types of bacteria that might be present. They grow and analyze the bacteria in petri dishes (above).

PLAYING A VITAL ROLE

Decades of the misuse of antibiotics cannot be reversed, but getting the message across about the right way to use these valuable drugs may at least help limit some of the damage in the future. And this is where we can all play our part.

TAKING ACTION

Over the past few years there have been public information campaigns in different countries about the dangers of inappropriate antibiotic use. However, the message has still not reached many people. Rates of antibiotic resistance have been found to be higher in southern European countries such as Greece and Spain, and lowest in Scandinavian countries. In the USA, the FDA has teamed up with the Centers for Disease Control to create a campaign called 'Get Smart: Know When Antibiotics Work'. This campaign aims to educate the public about when it is best to take antibiotics.

Everyone should follow simple rules:

- Most common infections are caused by viruses, not bacteria. Do not ask your doctor to prescribe an antibiotic unless you have a bacterial infection.
- Always take the drug in exactly the way it is set out by the doctor. If you do not finish the course, you are only killing off the weakest bacteria and allowing the stronger ones to flourish and fight back.
- Never take antibiotics that have been prescribed for someone else.
- Avoid using too many antibacterial products in your home. Ordinary soap and water are better than antibacterial soaps, which may help resistance in the environment.
- Wash your hands thoroughly as a matter of course to curb the spread of infections.

Antibiotics may do patients more harm than good if they are taken but not needed.

A CAREER IN SCIENCE

Stuart Levy is Professor of Molecular Biology and Microbiology and Director of the Center for Adaptation Genetics and Drug Resistance at Tufts University School of Medicine in Boston, Massachusetts, USA. He is the author of the best-selling book *The Antibiotic Paradox*, now in its second edition, which was key in alerting the world to the dangers of antibiotic misuse when it was first published in 1992. In 1981, he set up the Alliance for the Prudent Use of Antibiotics (APUA).

A DAY IN THE LIFE OF ...

Professor Levy's work is split between the Center for Adaptation Genetics and Drug Resistance at Tufts, the APUA and a role at a drug company called Paratek Pharmaceuticals. He founded the company and his research is key to work on new drugs and treatments for resistant pathogens. Professor Levy occasionally appears on television and in newspaper and magazine articles.

THE SCIENTIST SAYS ...

"It is vital that we appreciate the global picture of resistance. At the APUA, our goal is to bring resources to countries so they can do high quality testing. We mustn't lose the 'black boxes' that are out there, particularly in African countries lacking resources."

The MRSA bacterium is usually brought into the hospital by visitors – around 30 per cent of the population carry it naturally in their bodies.

FIGHTING MRSA

The superbug MRSA (see pages 28–9) is a major problem in the USA and recent figures from the Centers for Disease Control (CDC) show that 90,000 deaths are caused by it every year. About one in 20 Americans will pick up a hospital-acquired infection of this kind, but states are not required by law to report the figures. One study found that up to 60 per cent of these infections are resistant to the first line antibiotics that are used to treat them. The CDCs have launched a range of measures to try to curb the spread of MRSA, including awareness campaigns and monitoring of cases.

TAKING ACTION

In some parts of Europe, hospitals have been required by law to report all cases of MRSA. Many hospitals carry information reminding patients and visitors about the importance of hand washing. This is because MRSA is not only caused by a lack of hygiene on the part of doctors and nurses – it is often carried in people's systems. However, it makes sense that having strict rules about washing hands will help to

▶▶ www.mayoclinic.com/health/hand-washing/HQ00407

cut the spread of an infection. Even the ties that some doctors wear have been found to be a potential source of infection.

If you visit someone in hospital, you may see posters reminding visitors about the importance of hand washing. This is especially necessary for the most vulnerable patients, such as those in intensive care. Dispensers of alcohol rubs, which can kill bacteria, are also positioned outside most hospital wards and visitors are encouraged to use them before entering.

There are alcohol rubs at the foot of many hospital beds, especially in intensive care.

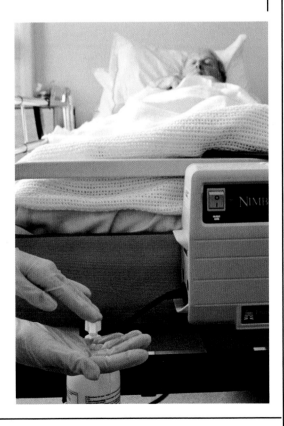

INVESTIGATING THE EVIDENCE: NEW ENZYMES

The investigation: The team looked at a new antibiotic called simocyclinone that is a good target for antibacterial action.

The scientists: Professor Tony Maxwell, Mr Marcus Edwards, Dr David Lawson, Ms Lesley Mitchenall, Dr Mark Buttner, Dr Clare Stephenson, Mr Tung Le (all at the John Innes Centre, Norwich, UK), Dr Tom Clarke (University of East Anglia, Norwich, UK), Dr Adam McKay (University College London, UK), Dr Hans-Peter Fiedler (University of Tubingen, Germany).

Gathering the evidence: The team targetted an enzyme, DNA gyrase, which is essential in all bacteria. They took purified simocyclinone from soil bacteria and then made crystals that were exposed to a powerful X-ray. This revealed how the drug binds to the enzyme and showed how it works.

The conclusion: The team discovered that simocyclinone knocks out DNA gyrase by a completely new mechanism. The team hopes this discovery will enable other scientists to develop future clinical antibiotics to exploit this discovery.

CHAPTER SEVEN

LOOKING TO THE FUTURE

AFTER DECADES OF COMPLACENCY ABOUT THE ROLE OF MEDICINES IN FIGHTING INFECTIOUS DISEASE, SCIENCE IS LOOKING FOR NEW WAYS TO COMBAT DRUG-RESISTANT MICROBES. WITH TUBERCULOSIS (TB) AT LEAST, THERE MAY BE HOPE ON THE HORIZON FOR FUTURE TREATMENTS.

GLOBAL ACTION

In 2006, a new global effort to attack TB was announced at the World Economic Forum meeting at Davos in Switzerland. The Global Plan to Stop TB is ambitious – it wants to halve the number of yearly deaths to one million by 2015. It also aimed to have the first new drug in the last 40 years, now estimated to be available around 2015. The aim is also to improve treatment programmes for up to 50 million people worldwide. Funding for the programme comes from charitable bodies such as the UK Department for International Development and the US Agency for International Development, as well as the governments of countries where TB is a major health problem. Despite an increase in this funding, it is still short of around $1bn.

TESTING METHODS

Currently, patients are tested for TB by a method that has been around for more than 125 years and has a failure rate of 50 per cent. It is known as the **sputum** test. This involves producing sputum, which is any mucus-like material that can be coughed up, and then analyzing it under a microscope to look for the mycobacterium that causes TB. According to WHO, only 2 per cent of MDR-TB (multi-drug resistant TB) cases worldwide are diagnosed and treated appropriately. There are many new tests under development.

DIAGNOSIS AND VACCINATION

A very accurate new test that diagnoses TB via its genetic makeup in under two hours will soon be available in Europe. It is relatively cheap so it could offer real hope in developing countries. Vaccines are also key to any future success and the first to reach the human testing stage in 80 years is now being trialled in South Africa. The current vaccine, BCG, has been in use since 1921 and around 3 billion people have been vaccinated. The main problem is that its effects run out after about ten years.

Here a macrophage – the BCG strain of the bacteria used in vaccinations – engulfs *Mycobacterium bovis* bacteria (orange), which causes tuberculosis.

Here, freeze-dried bovine vaccinations are being examined and stored in an animal laboratory. The vaccinations can be stored without deteriorating for a long time.

RESISTANCE AND HIV/AIDS

In 2005, HIV/AIDS reached a record figure of 40 million people worldwide. It has now overtaken the Black Death of the 14th century as the worst pandemic in human history. More than 60 per cent of the total number of infected people live in sub-Saharan Africa, and in some countries there, it has brought the life expectancy of an individual down to just 34 years of age.

One of the key goals in fighting HIV/AIDS is the development of an effective vaccine. Over the last 20 years, there have been several dozen projects around the world working on vaccines, and more money has been spent on this than on any other vaccine research in medical history. A vaccine to the virus remains elusive and some scientists doubt that one will be found, because of the virus' ability to replicate.

OLD AND NEW APPROACHES

Many different approaches are being taken, including those based on gene therapy, where faulty or damaged genes are replaced with healthy ones. The International AIDS Vaccine Initiative is a non-profit organization that is promoting research around the world. It claims that a record number of people are currently involved in clinical trials. At present, there are 18 drugs in 40 different strengths in Europe that are approved for HIV/AIDS treatment. Combinations of these drugs, in Highly Active Anti-Retroviral Therapy (or HAART) has been an effective therapy for the last 15 years, albeit in a drug regime that has side-effects and may be difficult to bear. According to the American Pharmacists' Association, up to 16 per cent of patients are resistant to at least one of the anti-retroviral drugs. Research over recent years has focused more on refining existing drugs than finding new ones, and there have been few brand new medicines released onto the market.

This test tube indicates that the blood inside has tested negative for HIV/AIDS.

A CAREER IN SCIENCE

Immunologist Dr David Margolis works at the Michael Hooker Research Center at the University of North Carolina, USA. The centre is a state-of-the-art research facility but also a clinical setting for real patients. Margolis realized while he was still at medical school that he had an interest in research, and chose to specialize in virology. He is now involved in HIV research, looking into the molecular mechanisms of the virus in order to produce more effective treatments.

A DAY IN THE LIFE OF …

Margolis spends most of the week analyzing data at the computer, but also works in the laboratory, culturing cells in incubators and observing the mechanisms of the virus at work. Because the centre is also a working medical facility, patients are directly involved in trying out any new treatments.

THE SCIENTIST SAYS …

"The first priority is to make sure that the patients are not harmed. That's always challenging, because while two mice are always the same, two people never are. When you are better able to understand how a virus works, and can use that knowledge to improve the health of people, that's very exciting."

There have been many different approaches to tackling malaria over the years, from attacking the mosquitos that carry the disease, to vaccination programmes and treatment.

PREVENTING MALARIA

The toll of malaria on children alone has been likened to seven packed jumbo jets crashing every single day. Over 100 years since the *Plasmodium falciparum* microbe responsible was first identified, are we any closer to finding a way to beat it?

Several malaria vaccine trials are being developed, but registration of a product is still many years away. There are more than a dozen different projects around the world that are working on a malaria vaccine. The biggest hopes lie with Artemisinin, to which the parasite has not yet become resistant. Elsewhere, a combination of two different anti-malarials in a drug called Coartem has been licensed for use by the US Food and Drug Administration with a 96 per cent success rate.

There is also research being conducted into the mosquito itself and how its genetics, physiology and **ecology** can be used to find new ways to treat, prevent or control the disease. One example is the possibility of genetically engineering mosquitoes that would be incapable of carrying the infectious parasite. This may involve inserting genes into mosquitoes to stop the parasite from developing.

In a strange twist on the debate about antibacterial products and their role in promoting microbial resistance, studies have shown that impregnating household surfaces with a type of fungus may help to curb the spread of the disease. The challenge now is to develop this technology into an inexpensive product.

A child in Tanzania, Africa, is vaccinated against malaria.

A CAREER IN SCIENCE

Paediatric parasite expert Dr Michele Spring works at the Walter Reed Army Institute of Research at Silver Spring in Maryland, USA. After graduating in parasitology, she joined the Peace Corps in West Africa, where she travelled to small villages to help combat a disease called guinea worm. She qualified as a paediatrician with an interest in how children are affected by parasitic disease. She is now involved in malaria vaccine research.

A DAY IN THE LIFE OF ...

Dr Spring spends most of her time in the office or clinic, organizing studies to test malaria vaccines in volunteers. She helps give out the new malaria vaccines, follows the volunteers to see if the vaccine has any side-effects, and also takes blood to see how the volunteers' immune systems react to the vaccine. Sometimes, volunteers are given malaria by mosquito bite to see if the vaccine protects them against the disease. One day, Dr Spring hopes that a vaccine tested in the clinic will be available to help young children in Africa.

THE SCIENTIST SAYS ...

"What inspires me about this research is the chance that this work may reduce the threat of malaria infection and disease from certain parts of the world, and that children more susceptible to malaria can grow up healthy and strong."

Pollution from sewage and chemicals does enormous damage to the environment and may encourage bacteria in their resistance to antibiotics (see box right).

THE ROGUE'S GALLERY OF MICROBES

Most of the bacteria, fungi and viruses referred to in this book are well known. A group of scientists working with the Infectious Diseases Society of America has come up with a list of microbial villains that should be given the highest priority in terms of research because of the scarcity of medicines to treat them. The list includes MRSA, but also the following:

- *Acinetobacter baumannii*: the fungus behind hospital-acquired pneumonia cases and infections in wounded US soldiers.
- *Escherichia coli* (*E. coli*) and *Klebsiella*: cause infections in the urinary tract, gut and wounds.
- Aspergillus: a fungal infection that plagues people with poorly working immune systems such as those with HIV, cancer or organ transplants, and kills 50–60 per cent of those it infects.
- Vancomycin-resistant *Enterococcus faecium*: a bug responsible for infections of the bloodstream, heart and brain, among others.
- *Pseudomonas aeruginosa*: a life-threatening bacterium that

E. coli can get into your stomach and intestines via undercooked beef.

particularly affects patients with the lung disease cystic fibrosis.

Alongside these top six, other microbes have shown increasing resistance in recent years. These include the following:

- *Shigella dysenteria (S. dysenteria)*: a form of dysentery that is a deadly infection in the developing world, killing many children.
- *Streptococcus pneumoniae (S. pneumoniae)*: causes pneumonia.
- *Haemophilus influenzae*: this can cause meningitis in young children.
- *Neisseria gonorrhoea*: a bacterium that is responsible for the sexually transmitted disease gonorrhoea.

INVESTIGATING THE EVIDENCE: IS POLLUTION DRIVING RESISTANCE?

The investigation: Scientists are researching the possibility that pollution from sewage sludge, animal slurry, disinfectants and fabric softeners is linked to the way that bacteria are resisting the effects of antibiotics.

The scientists: Dr William Gaze, Professor Elizabeth Wellington and Dr Lihong Zhang from Warwick University, UK, working with Professor Peter Hawkey from Birmingham University, UK.

Gathering the evidence: The team gathered samples from areas of land where pollution was present and compared them with nearby soil and against samples that had had no contact with pollutants. The samples were frozen to minus 80 degrees and studied in the laboratory using molecular DNA analysis.

The conclusion so far: The millions of tonnes of sewage sludge and animal slurry spread on land every year contain resistant bacteria. The team found that this process is causing bacteria-carrying genetic elements that help resistance genes to get into soil and water.

WHERE DO WE GO FROM HERE?

The view that humans could conquer or dominate the world of microbes is looking at best optimistic and at worst arrogant in the second decade of the 21st century. Despite huge advances in medical science, common infections still kill millions of people, particularly in the developing world.

During the last three decades of the 20th century, drug companies targeted problems such as cancer, diabetes and heart disease, instead of developing new drugs. But the realization of the threat from resistant microbes has been heightened by the threat of a biological terrorist attack. More money is now being targeted at finding new ways to beat bacteria.

NEW IDEAS

Genetic engineering is being explored as one way to make bacteria more susceptible to existing drugs, and there is new research into an older technique involving antibodies. Antibodies are the body's own defence against invasion, and they are found in serum, a component of blood. Serum therapy was used before antibiotics were developed, but there were side-effects and toxic reactions. However, with the modern-day understanding of genetics and immunity, scientists have been able to update this therapy with some success. A drug called Synagis, which uses serum therapy to target a virus that causes serious respiratory infection in young children, is now in use.

Scientists are exploring many new avenues to tackle the problem of drug resistance. Over time, we can expect to see new drugs and treatments on the market. But will what we have learned about nature's ability to fight back be taken seriously in the future? The world is waking up to the fact that humans are just part of a complex and unimaginably diverse range of life that is struggling to survive on this planet. We may have to re-think our belief in our own superiority if we are to continue to hold our own.

Human serum contains salts, glucose and other proteins, including antibodies formed by the body's immune system to fight infection.

AART Active Anti-Retroviral Therapy, a treatment for HIV/AIDS

antibiotics a medicine or chemical that can destroy harmful bacteria in the body

chemotherapy the treatment of diseases using chemicals

commensal describes a relationship among two or more species, in which one or both species benefit from the other without causing harm

DDT an insecticide once widely used to repel malarial mosquitoes

derivative a substance or compound obtained from another substance or compound

disease illness of humans, animals, plants, etc., caused by infection

DNA deoxyribonucleic acid, the chemical at the centre of the cells of living things

E. coli a bacterium that normally lives in the human colon; most strains are harmless but some are very dangerous

ecology the relationship between organisms and their environment

evolution the way in which living things change and develop over periods of time

fungus any of various types of organism that get their food from decaying material or living things

genome the complete set of genetic material of a human, animal, plant or other living thing

HIV/AIDS the human immunodeficiency virus (HIV) infects cells of the immune system, destroying or impairing their function. Acquired immunodeficiency syndrome (AIDS) describes the most advanced stages of HIV infection

immunity being protected against the damaging effects of disease

latent present but symptomless infection by a pathogen

lymphatic system part of the immune system, it helps the body fight infections

malaria a disease caused by a parasite that is transmitted from one human to another by the bite of infected *Anopheles* mosquitoes

MDR-TB Multi-Drug Resistant TB, which is resistant to a variety of the drugs usually used to treat it

microbe a very tiny form of life such as bacteria, fungi and protozoan parasites

microbiologist a person who studies the microbes that cause infectious disease

microscope an instrument that uses lenses to produce magnified images of objects too small to be seen by the eye

mould all species of microscopic, multicellular fungi; those that grow as single cells are called yeasts

MRSA Methicillin-resistant *Staphylococcus aureus* are a type of staphylococcus or 'staph' bacteria that is resistant to many antibiotics

mutation a permanent change in genetic material

nutrient any substance that is taken in by organisms and promotes growth

organism any living thing that can survive independently

pathogen any microbe that can cause disease

plasmid a small, circular piece of DNA, found in bacteria and yeasts, that is able to replicate independently

protozoa a group of one-celled animals, some of which cause human diseases such as malaria

replication the reproduction of something by making an exact copy

resistant the condition of an organism that means that it can resist a disease or a drug

respiratory system the organs that are involved in breathing

side-effects unwanted effects from taking a medicine

sputum mucus and other material produced by the lining of the respiratory tract – also called phlegm; a sputum test is used to test for tuberculosis

therapeutic concerned with the treatment of disease

tuberculosis (TB) a highly infectious disease that is caused by the organism *Mycobacterium tuberculosis*

vaccine a biological preparation that improves immunity to a particular disease

virus a microscopic infectious agent that replicates itself only within cells of living hosts and cannot survive independently

WHO the World Health Organization – a United Nations agency that coordinates international health activities, and helps governments improve health services worldwide

yeast any of various small, single-celled fungi